The Shortest Book on Marriage

RICH BULLOCK
SHERYL BULLOCK

REDDING, CALIFORNIA

Contents

PART ONE
SIMPLE

The Most Basic Concept   3
1. Do this...   5
2. The big secret   13
3. It's all about ME   15
4. Make me happy   17
5. We get along, so what's the problem?   19
6. So...   21

PART TWO
DEEPER CONCEPTS

7. Vows & Commitment   27
8. Risking everything   31

PART THREE
IT'S PERSONAL

9. Your Stories   37
10. The Learning Curve - Rich   39
11. The Learning Curve - Sheryl   43
The end - (seriously)   47

To readers   49
Also by the authors   50
About the authors   51

The Shortest Book on Marriage

Our deepest desire

is to love and be loved

in a way that risks everything.

— V.M. Narrano, *Beyond Us:*
The Writings of V.M. Narrano

Part One

SIMPLE

The Most Basic Concept

The idea came to me (Rich) one night after talking to a couple in crisis. I realized they were not doing a single thing to move *toward* each other. That had me looking at my own marriage. (Gulp!)

And while there are many excellent books on marriage, they are typically long and thoroughly cover topics, providing tools for going deeper.

Great...except, as one advance reader of *The Shortest Book on Marriage* put it, "Most marriage books *wear you out*."

Sometimes all we need is a reminder of the most basic concept.

Here we go...

1. Do this...

Do something that brings you together in your marriage...

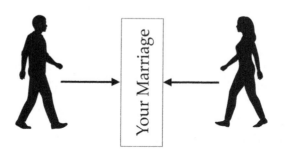

...every day.

Don't do this...

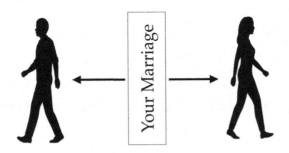

...EVER!

Got it?

Good.

~ The End ~

Well...
maybe that's too simple.

Here's a little more.

Don't walk away from daily relationship...

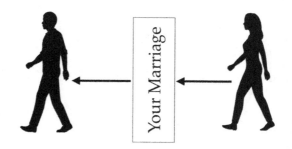

...EVER.

Either spouse can play this game.

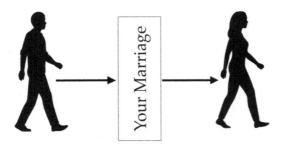

No one wins...

...EVER.

Uh... Nope.

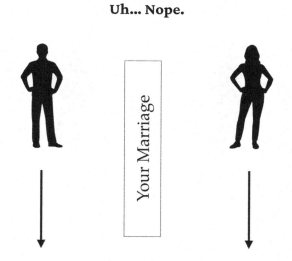

Separate lives together is not a marriage.

Drifting apart is a no-win...

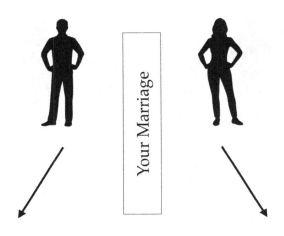

Your Marriage

...so

don't.

2. The big secret

Marriage is simple in concept, right? Two people joined together. It's even biblical and often included in wedding vows.

> *"That is why a man leaves his father and mother and is united to his wife, and they become one flesh."*

GENESIS 2:24

Pretty clear. However, that *one flesh* unit is still made up of two individuals who bring years (or decades) of baggage to the happily-ever-after ideal.

So here's the big secret...

You have to...

Do something every day that brings you together.

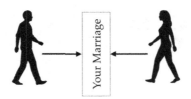

Otherwise, you'll gradually drift apart.

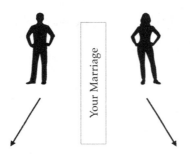

Guaranteed.

3. It's all about ME

Selfish vs Selfless

A sel*fish* partner demands his or her personal rights and desires, and focuses on what the other person can or should do for them.

A sel*fless* partner sets aside their own personal rights and desires, and builds up their spouse.

Selfish doesn't work.
Will never work.
Can't work.

So just stop, okay?

4. Make me happy

Giver vs Taker

If you expect your partner to make you happy (and, at some level, we all do when we begin dating and are first married), you'll be disappointed. Because love is an action of *giving* to the other person.

This is why the arrows point to your spouse.

He gives to her.

She gives to him.

Marriage is both people
<u>Giving</u> and both <u>Receiving</u>.
It's not one Giving and the other Taking.

5. We get along, so what's the problem?

Parallel Existence

It's sometimes called the "roommate marriage." But perhaps "non-marriage" is a better definition, because it's two people cooperating side by side.

Two career-oriented or self-oriented people who got married but never gave up their separate lives. They have their own social groups, bank accounts, cars, and activities. Kids might be in the picture.

Day-to-day is predominantly transactional. They decide on *things*: groceries, housekeeping, bills. But they are not growing closer as a couple. They might even have sex, 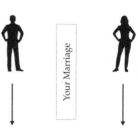 but their relationship isn't really "one flesh" in soul and spirit. Their individual lives are a barrier to truly joining together.

This cannot stand. If they don't do something to grow toward each other each day, they will drift further and further apart.

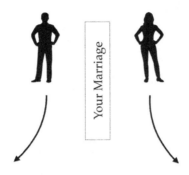

Your Marriage

6. So...

Do something every day that brings you together.

It might be a hug, a kiss, a thanks, or an "I'll do that for you."

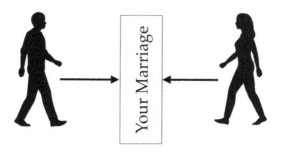

Men: "You look nice" or "you crushed it!" works. But don't wait for her to ask—you have to be the one who notices. And don't "phone it in" with a quick glance at her and then go back to your sports show or computer game. That's not really *walking toward her*, is it. Get off the couch, ditch your cell, and concentrate on her. Put in some effort.

Women: "I'm proud of you" or "I married a smart man" always makes a guy feel good. Remember, almost every man feels like a poser and fears he'll be found out to be a fraud—because he doesn't know half of what he's doing most of the time. Seriously.

Your respect gives him confidence, makes him want to open up and be a better man and better husband.

Start making your own list of ways you can move together:

1. Compliments (see above)
2. Chocolate on his or her pillow (Unexpected!)
3. Wash his or her car (they'll brag to their friends)
4. Fold the laundry (guys: big points with this one, especially if you put it away)
5. Back rub
6. Ask friends what they do to move toward their spouse. You'll encourage them to up their game!
7. Add to your list every day, because you'll use them up fast!

That's the simple concept.
Move toward each other—every day.

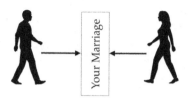

You can do this!

The End

Really.

Well, actually this is the end of the simple concept.

But there's more.

Part Two

DEEPER CONCEPTS

F. Vows & Commitment

Actress Audrey Hepburn famously said:

"If I get married, I want to be very married."

Great quote. Well, she did marry—twice. And she divorced—twice. And both she and her second husband had affairs while married. Oops.

From her words above, she *wanted* to get it right and make it last, but couldn't manage it. Unfortunately, that happens to many couples.

Some people hedge their bets right from the beginning. Instead of *"...until death do us part,"* have you heard the following vow spoken at a wedding ceremony?

"As long as we both shall love."

Sorry if this was part of your vows, but let me explain why that isn't the best way to pledge yourself to your new spouse. It feels like *"I don't expect this to last. Maybe (probably) one of us will find someone better, or you'll annoy me until I can no longer tolerate you."*

In other words, if love disappears, I'm outta here. Yeah, that's a serious commitment right there, because there will always be periods where love cools.

What if...

You're a young soldier at war, crouching at the front line, with the enemy 50 yards away across a perilous clearing. Your buddy is at your side. Orders are to advance.

"Let's do this," you say, knowing you'll never make it across without your partner's support.

He says, "I'm right with you."

You rise to your feet, scale the trench wall, and prepare to charge.

Then he adds, "Unless it gets too hard. Or dangerous. Or not fun. Or if I'm not feeling fulfilled."

— 😶 ??!!

At a wedding, a vow based on the scenario above might be: *"I promise to love you—unless things get tough. Then I'll run away and leave you on your own."*

What we desire to hear is:

"I promise to love you and always be by your side, through all the ups and downs."

Vows should inspire trust to grow larger, not shrink. If not, or if they are easily broken or tossed aside, they are empty words and not worth much.

Move toward each other every day and you'll build trust, confidence, and freedom, knowing that mistakes will be forgiven.

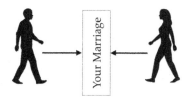

"Before our family and friends, for richer or poorer, in sickness and in health, for better or worse, I promise to love you and spend the rest of my days with you."

Now *that* is what a vow *and the marriage* should be...in *deeds*, not only in words.

Whoever you marry should say those words to you and mean them. Don't settle for less.

You should mean them too.

8. Risking everything

Our deepest desire
is to love and be loved
in a way that risks everything.

Most of us don't risk without first trusting the other person. If that other person doesn't *have* our back, we will *hold* back.

In a poker game, it's called *holding (or playing) your cards close to your vest*, or not *tipping your hand*. It means revealing as little as possible to the person across the table, who is an <u>opponent</u>, not a <u>partner</u>. Your goal is to beat them and drag the pile of chips to your side. To win.

That's not true in marriage—at least it better not be. Marriage should be a safe environment of trust, where each partner is willing to show their cards and speak their secret fears, hurts, hopes, dreams, and desires.

You are a team of two, and positive support by your partner builds deep trust. This is what intimacy is about.

It's moving toward each other—every day.

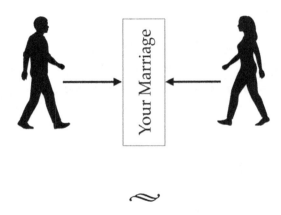

Part Three

IT'S PERSONAL

9. Your Stories

One fun way to move toward each other is by writing your stories of how you came to be a couple and some of your first experiences. Differing views of the same memory make for interesting discussions!

Don't attempt a 300 page memoir. It's far better to do this in short vignettes—a few paragraphs. Not really a writer? Pretend you're telling the story at a party or around a dinner table.

Ideas

- First time you met: Across a crowded room. College. Hated each other on meeting. In church—maybe still hated each other! :-)
- What attracted you to him or her?
- A memorable date—or a disaster date to forget.

- Impressing the in-laws the first time (or not).
- A time when everything went wrong.
- The wedding. The good, the bad, and the...oops.
- Life challenges.

Keep these positive, even if the situation was troubling —or worse. The best will include what *you* learned yourself, or what you learned together. Our personal examples follow in the next chapters.

10. The Learning Curve - Rich

Sheryl and I married on Friday the 13th. Yep. We had no trouble reserving the church, photographer, flowers, and cake. Everyone was available!

Some probably thought we were crazy—not because of the superstition regarding the day, but because we were both 21 years old and had only the vaguest idea of what was to come. So true.

My dad paid for my college tuition and room & board the first three years, but with my senior year beginning, I was now a married man and expected to provide for myself and my new wife. No pressure.

Fortunately, Dad gave us some money as a wedding present, which helped a great deal when the engine on our 1965 Mustang failed a few weeks into the fall semester (Swapping the engine in a friend's driveway in a marathon all-nighter is a story in itself).

Dad and Mom grew up during the Great Depression. The expectation was for us to "step up" to the challenge of becoming an adult. By "expectation" I mean that was *our* thinking—Sheryl and me. I'm not sure what Dad and Mom thought—we didn't talk much about those things back then. Sheryl and I were in Dallas, far from family homes in California, and we learned fast to be independent and a team.

Here's what I learned:

Teamwork: It was the two of us against adversity. Whether car repairs, finding jobs, paying our rent on time, or dealing with disappointments during our new marriage, we learned that life is a lot of work, and tackling those responsibilities builds character that lasts a lifetime. So much more to this, but it's character that's carried us beyond 50 years together.

Support: We were (and are) each other's #1 cheerleader. When I was down, she shouted encouragement, and I did the same for her. And if something more catastrophic happened—real trouble—we held each other up. You don't walk away.

Companionship: When you're poor, and we were— we had no house phone because of cost, and cell phones were still years in the future—you find cheap things to do. Dollar movie nights; low-cost eats; games with friends; a day at the local lake. No cable TV, so we spent a lot of time talking and forging our life together. Distractions in this area can eat young marriages alive. ***We were fortunate to be poor.***

Finances: We pooled our money (no separate checking accounts with each paying their "fair share" and that sort of thing), and we decided together where to spend it. Over the years, we put yet another motor in that old Mustang (plus 5 clutches and a self-done paint job that was, I admit, simply awful), and drove it 250,000 miles. Later, our 1984 Toyota van ran up 272,000 miles. I've learned to listen to Sheryl. If she's not comfortable with a purchase or investment, I back off (I'm a little slow, so it took me a while). And she's become bolder in voicing her opinions. I guess finances and communication go hand in hand.

Intimacy: (both physically and intellectually) requires constant work. Make it a priority. It's worth it. Never stop. Just sayin'.

Challenge: Perhaps the best thing we do is challenge each other to do better and try new things. That goes back to Cheerleading 101. Sheryl still challenges me to be better. She doesn't do it by nagging. She continually improves herself, and I have to run to catch up.

You'll notice "Love" isn't on the list. Because it's actually the *ENTIRE* list. The feelings come and go, and sometimes we do better at expressing those feelings than at other times, but the <u>actions</u> of love go on and on. They are the glue because we're <u>focused</u> on the other person.

You'll also notice "Kids" aren't on the list. Why? Get this, because it is super important:

> *We fell in love and chose each other long before children came into the picture.*

Kids don't define us. Our relationship with each other is primary and has been from day one.

And all these years later (after the kids are out of the house), we're still choosing each other, functioning as a team, building intimacy, and challenging each other to do better, be better.

I'm so grateful to have a loving best friend and partner who I see every day.

11. The Learning Curve - Sheryl

Choosing: Rich chose me. It is many a woman's greatest fear that no one will choose her. I know we live in a world where women choose men. But I believe deep inside a woman is the desire that she will be wanted and chosen by a man. Women are made to be lovingly pursued. And a man needs to know he's done the work to win her heart.

Healing: Marriage is a place of healing for me. It was designed for this...for safety, transparency, and a different kind of love not found in our backgrounds or our families of origin. This kind of love is unique to marriage, yet many people never discover it. None of us come into this union unscathed. Despite having a "good" childhood, we all have insecurities, blind spots, and weaknesses. Marriage is created to be a place of security, where both people rise up and grow individually and together.

Conflict: You learn to do battle well. I didn't know how to have a good fight. If my parents disagreed, I never saw it, so I went into marriage thinking you should avoid disagreement. I had to learn to speak up, to value my opinion, to risk being misunderstood or possibly even rejected. This skill is something that, when undeveloped, leads to a passive, lifeless marriage. Conflict, when it's attached to love, can actually strengthen marriage.

Sex is Body & Soul: You learn how to express love physically. Sex is complicated because it's attached to our whole being. The mechanics of intercourse can happen, but our deepest self can hide in the shadows, "unseen" by our mate. As we move into wholeness, sex becomes a combination of physical and spiritual joy. It's a crazy good thing not found anywhere else in the human existence. It's about body and soul. It's also about having a sense of humor.

Spiritual: We encourage each other in our relationship with God. Rich and I have very different styles of how we connect with God. How we read and study the Bible and how we converse with God is not the same. We've given each other the freedom to do what works best for each of us without casting an expectation over each other. At the end of each day, we can pray together and talk about how God reached out to us.

Selfless: It's not about me....as we mentioned earlier in the book. I learn sacrifice, service, and forgiveness through marriage. This is the greatest revelation about marriage, and it's why many don't make it past a few years. Marriage is about loving my mate well.

The end –
(seriously)

Our society demands dozens of decisions each week, everything from choosing between a *non-fat venti pumpkin spiced latte no whip*, or two burgers at In-n-Out (about the same price), or how to pay for a new roof with only $300 in the bank.

A strong marriage is a tremendous advantage. Read these wise words from Ecclesiastes 4:9-12 (NLT):

> *Two people are better off than one, for they can help each other succeed. If one person falls, the other can reach out and help. But someone who falls alone is in real trouble. Likewise, two people lying close together can keep each other warm. But how can one be warm alone? A person standing alone can be attacked and defeated, but two can stand back-to-back and conquer.*

**Do something that brings
you together in your marriage...
...every day!**

The End

To readers

Thanks for reading **The Shortest Book on Marriage**. Even though it's brief, we hope you'll remember the basic concept of moving toward each other every day.

If you enjoyed the book, please consider writing a review. In the spirit of things, keep it short!

We'd love to hear directly, too. Email us at...

rich@perilousfiction.com

Blessings to you as we journey through this life together!

— Rich & Sheryl Bullock

Also by the authors

Books by Rich Bullock

Perilous Safety Series
Perilous Cove

Storm Song

Desperation Falls

Glass & Stone Series
Shattered Glass

Glass Revenge

Killing Callie

Lake Effect Series
Night Skyy

Nonfiction (sort of)
Beyond Us: The Writings of V.M. Narrano

Wild Life: The Writings of V.M. Narrano

Children's book by Sheryl Bullock
The Journey of the Doll Cradle

About the authors

Rich Bullock usually writes suspense novels of ordinary people put in perilous situations where lives change forever. But once in a while he goes off the rails and writes something practical.

Growing up in small-town San Luis Obispo, California, gave him an affinity for settings that remind people of home.

Sheryl Bullock is a life coach, mentor, and children's book author. She has a passion for strengthening young marriages, and encourages parents and grandparents to share their love and wisdom with the next generation.

She enjoys camping and hiking and is especially proud of climbing 10,457 foot Mount Lassen.

Riding The Carousel of Happiness, Nederland, Colorado. https://www.carouselofhappiness.org/

Rich and Sheryl live in Redding, California, and have been married over 50 years. They are still practicing moving toward each other...every day!

www.perilousfiction.com
rich@perilousfiction.com

facebook.com/perilousfiction

twitter.com/richwords

Made in the USA
Las Vegas, NV
07 December 2022

61385388R00037